What Research Says to the Teacher

English as a Second Language
by Christina Bratt Paulston

National Education Association
Washington, D.C.

PE
1128
A2
P33

Copyright © 1980
National Education Association of the United States

Stock No. 1051-5-00

Note
The opinions expressed in this publication should not be construed as representing the policy or position of the National Education Association. Materials published as part of the What Research Says to the Teacher series are intended to be discussion documents for teachers who are concerned with specialized interests of the profession.

Library of Congress Cataloging in Publication Data
Paulston, Christina Bratt, 1932-
  English as a second language.
  (What research says to the teacher)
  Bibliography: p.
  1. English language—Study and teaching—Foreign students. I. Title. II. Series.
PE1128.A2P33   428'.007   80-19050
ISBN 0-8106-1051-5

CONTENTS

INTRODUCTION 5

THE HISTORICAL DEVELOPMENT OF TESOL IN THE
    UNITED STATES 6

THE DOMAINS OF TESOL 10
    English as a Foreign Language (EFL) 10
    English as a Second Language (ESL) 11
    Bilingual Education (BE) 11
    English to Speakers of Other Dialects (ESOD) 16

WHO TEACHES WHAT TO WHOM FOR WHAT PURPOSE TO
    WHAT EFFECT 17
    Who—the Teachers 17
    What—the Subject 19
    Whom—the Students 24
    For What Purpose—Objectives 27
    To What Effect—Methods and Techniques 28

CONCLUSION 34

SELECTED REFERENCES 35

The Author

Christina Bratt Paulston is Professor of Linguistics, Chair of the Department of General Linguistics, and Co-Director of the English Language Institute at the University of Pittsburgh. She is the author of numerous publications, including *Write on: A Program in Controlled Composition* and *Bilingual Education: Issues and Theories;* as well as a frequent contributor to professional journals.

The Consultants

The following educators have reviewed the manuscript and provided helpful comments and suggestions:

James E. Alatis, Dean and Professor of Linguistics, School of Languages and Linguistics, Georgetown University, Washington, D.C.

Mary Newton Bruder, Lecturer in Linguistics and Co-Director of the English Language Institute, Department of General Linguistics, University of Pittsburgh

Betty Wallace Robinett, Professor of Linguistics and Acting Assistant Vice President of Academic Affairs, University of Minnesota

Muriel Saville-Troike, Associate Professor of Linguistics, School of Languages and Linguistics, Georgetown University, Washington, D.C.

INTRODUCTION

This publication is a discussion of what is known today about learning and teaching English as a second language, also known as TESOL (teaching English to speakers of other languages). By necessity, when one person attempts to interpret so diverse a field as TESOL and applied linguistics, there are bound to be conflicting views and interpretations of the same phenomena. It is important, then, for an accurate interpretation of my remarks that the reader understand the particular viewpoint from which I speak. I am in profound agreement with Abraham Kaplan's notion that there is nothing so practical as good theory, but the fact is that there is not a good theory for language learning. There are many theories from several disciplines which attempt to account for language learning and language teaching, and many of those theories are conflicting. But there is also knowledge about language learning and language teaching from an empirical approach, from trial and error in the classroom. As Director of an English Language Institute, which teaches English to academically oriented students, I am involved with the problems our students face daily. Their needs are the primary influence on my thinking about language teaching. Theoretical speculations are interesting, and it is very clear to me that a solid theoretical foundation is necessary for significant progress in understanding how languages are learned, but, for now, the approach taken here is that of the putative Missourian: "You've got to show me."

In other words, this book ignores or only briefly touches upon such theoretical issues in second language acquisition as those connected with morpheme acquisition studies and the critical period hypothesis, to mention just two topics. It deals instead with practical matters in and out of the classroom. This may be an unfashionable and unprestigious view in academia, but I feel reasonably certain from my own six years of teaching in the public schools that classroom teachers will understand the choice.

The book first sketches the historical development of the field and then discusses the domains of TESOL with special attention to bilingual education. The major part is concerned with who teaches what to whom for what purpose to what effect, to paraphrase Lazarsfeld's famous formula; i.e., with the teachers and the subject matter they teach, with the students and what they learn, and finally with how effectively this process is carried out—a how-to section.

THE HISTORICAL DEVELOPMENT OF TESOL IN THE UNITED STATES

Language teaching goes back almost as far as historical records. Before 2000 B.C. there is evidence of "important bilingual scribal schools in which the native Akkadian and the traditional Sumerian were taught" (61).* The prophet Daniel, selected for a scribal education by Nebuchadnezzar, was taught to communicate in languages other than his native Hebrew. There were Greek and Latin, both of which, at various times, were used as languages of wider communication (LWC) as well as of scholarly learning, and their influence in education remains to our own day long after the living languages are no more. Saint Augustine developed a dialogue method of teaching and Cicero advocated a form of controlled composition (50). There is in fact very little under the sun that has never been tried in language teaching. What does change are the answers to the question who teaches what to whom for what purpose. Presumably Nebuchadnezzar's concern for language teaching was not the same as that of the President's Commission on Foreign Language and International Studies (71). The historical development of TESOL is not just an account of scholarly thought in ivory towers; it is also and more importantly a reflection of social and political factors in the United States and the world.

What also changes are the combination and constellation of classroom techniques into the various methods as well as the theories which attempt to account for these methods. While it is true that most classroom techniques may have been tried at one time or another, the particular context in which they were tried and the rationale for trying them were different. At present TESOL is the scene of a number of competing methods to satisfy just about any taste, but this was not always the case.

The historical development of TESOL as a field of study in the United States is generally held to date from World War II and the so-called army method which became known variously in peacetime as the audiolingual approach, the aural-oral method, the mim-mem method, and sometimes the ESL method. But it is necessary to backtrack briefly to understand this development.

Until roughly the turn of the century all language study in Europe and the United States had been done with Latin as the model and Latin grammar as the mold for describing other languages. These Latinate grammars worked because the languages described were Indo-European

---

*Numbers in parentheses appearing in the text refer to the Selected References beginning on page 35.

and closely related to Latin. Occasionally silly prescriptions occurred, however. For example, infinitives cannot be split in Latin, so there is now the rule that infinitives should not be split in English. Because there is no linguistically valid reason for this rule in English, many linguists instead make it a rule to occasionally split their infinitives to prove their liberated point. (Editors then unsplit them right back.)

Then around the turn of the century, when cultural anthropologists began the serious study of the languages and cultures of American Indians, the Latinate grammars no longer served to describe these typologically very different languages. As Stuart points out, Franz Boas in his Introduction to the *Handbook of American Indian Languages* (11) marked "the beginning of American descriptive linguistics and the effective starting point of a new direction in grammatical studies" (99). In 1921, another anthropologist, Edward Sapir, published *Language: An Introduction to the Study of Speech* (85) which was to have great influence on thinking about language. Sapir's most influential idea, known as the Sapir-Whorf hypothesis (107), is that the structure of the language one speaks influences the way one perceives the world. (Although this is an attractive idea to nonlinguists, most linguists remain skeptical.) In 1933, Leonard Bloomfield published *Language* (10) which Bowen refers to as the bible of American structural linguistics, and indeed it is now possible to begin to talk about the discipline of linguistics, a very new field of study, oriented toward speech rather than writing (13).

Other scholars contributing to the development of structural linguistics in the United States were missionaries who, in groups like the Wycliffe Bible Translators and the Summer Institute of Linguistics, were dedicated to spreading the Word of God by translating the gospels into primarily unwritten languages. Partially, the very practical demands of translation influenced their thinking about linguistics. To give but one example: many languages have inclusive *we* ('all of us guys') and exclusive *we* ('my friend and I but not you guys'); and if such forms are unfamiliar, the inclusive/exclusive feature of the first person plural pronoun is far from immediately apparent. So it is not surprising that the missionaries inadvertently translated "Our Father" with exclusive *we*, and subsequently discovered to their horror the Aymara Indians' interpretation of a God for white folk only, which notion was the last on earth they had intended.

Accordingly, scholars like Kenneth Pike of the Summer Institute of Linguistics in his *Phonemics: A Technique for Reducing Languages to Writing* (75), Eugene Nida of the American Bible Society in his *Morphology: The Descriptive Analysis of Words* (68), and later H. A. Gleason of the Hartford Seminary Foundation in *An Introduction to Descriptive Linguistics* (38) were genuinely concerned with what came to be known as "discovery procedures," the analysis of unknown and unwritten languages.

This practical bent of anthropologists and missionaries in the development of American linguistics was important for two reasons. It contributed enormously to the knowledge about the world's languages other than the Indo-European group, and it inadvertently developed techniques for learning them through the focus on discovery procedures. With World War II and the need for a knowledge of strategic but obscure languages,* the United States Army found a gold mine in the linguists' expertise in languages never previously taught paired with the practical American know-how for learning them. Thus the Army Specialized Training Program was established to teach languages intensively to military personnel using native-speaking teachers, extensive contact, small classes, and high student motivation (13).

The results were considered excellent and the excellence attributed to the method. (It is legitimate to wonder now whether any method may not have had excellent results, given the motivation, the time, the money, and the expertise.) After the war the audiolingual method became firmly ensconced in the universities during the fifties and sixties. It is not clear to me how much of a role a theoretical rationale for language learning played in the development of the army language courses in those hectic war days, but the audiolingual approach, as expounded by structural linguists like Charles Fries (35), Robert Lado (54), and Nelson Brooks (14), was clearly and explicitly wedded to behaviorist psychology and reinforcement theory (80). The basic tenets of the audiolingual approach, as formulated in Moulton's five slogans of 1961, were as follows:

1. Language is speech, not writing.
2. A language is a set of habits.
3. Teach the language, not about the language.
4. A language is what native speakers say, not what someone thinks they ought to say.
5. Languages are different. (65)

As Prator discusses (76), not a single one of these slogans is not questioned today on theoretical grounds. In the fifties, however, they led to a method of teaching characterized by presentation of oral language before written, extensive pattern-practice and dialogue memorization, a minimum of explanations, and, many would add, exquisite tedium since students were never encouraged to say anything on their own for fear of making mistakes which would then become habit.

---
*Linguists eschew the term "exotic languages" on the grounds that no language is exotic to its mother tongue speakers. On the other hand, since one cannot comfortably talk about "the Less Commonly Taught Languages" all day, the fond in-house term is "the funny languages." Illogical? Of course!

All in all, there was a situation in which compelling social factors demanded the learning of English at the same time that a very questionable method for teaching it was in vogue. The emergence of the Allies as victors in World War II resulted in the even firmer establishment of English as the world language of trade and politics, in an economy which enabled the United States to play a leading role in world reconstruction—carried out mostly in English—and eventually in the establishment of the Peace Corps whose substantial if inadvertent contribution to English language teaching has been basically ignored. In addition, the United States faced simultaneously the problems of many displaced persons and political refugees who did not speak English and a strong ideology for conformity and America-as-the-melting-pot. More than once, as a foreign student in Minnesota in the early fifties, I was told when criticizing some feature of American life: "If you don't like it here, go back to where you came from." The pressure for immigrants to the United States to repress the mother tongue and to learn English to conform to mainstream values was enormous.

One would think that the audiolingual method could not stand up to such demands. Eventually it did not, but it did have a few points in its favor. The theoretical foundation on which the method was built was very solid. Today most linguists think it was an inadequate theory (theories are rarely wrong), but it is still perfectly possible for an inadequate theory to be solidly and elegantly argued. Many scholars gained national recognition as proponents of the audiolingual method, and this method is, of course, what they taught their students. Many readers of this book will have been trained in this method or will have studied a foreign language taught audiolingually. The other point in its favor was the Sputnik scare of the fifties which resulted in large amounts of federal monies becoming available for language teaching. Virtually all the National Defense Foreign Language Institutes established to "retool" teachers advocated the audiolingual method and helped disseminate it in the public schools.

It should be added that no sensible teacher was ever likely to actually teach according to the "pure" theoretical tenets of the audiolingual method, and with good teachers, so-called audiolingual courses were often successful. It is easy to criticize the method so completely that one throws out the baby with the bathwater, and that is not helpful.

The whole situation led to two developments. First, a profound distaste for the study of foreign languages occurred in the United States to the point that "Americans' incompetence in foreign languages is nothing short of scandalous, and it is becoming worse," according to the President's Commission on Foreign Language and International Studies (71). Clearly, social factors are more important in explaining this development, but I think the audiolingual method may have helped. Second, a group of people emerged, with academic training in the teaching of English to speakers of other languages, who strongly felt the need for a way to obtain professional recognition and outlet for their interests; for a professional organization which could contribute a sense of discipline, uniform standards, information, teacher qualification, and all those matters which make a profession a profession. In 1966, the TESOL organization was founded; with its affiliates today it numbers approximately twenty-five thousand members. TESOL has come of age as a profession in its own right.

THE DOMAINS OF TESOL

Because TESOL covers a multitude of teaching situations and students needs, this diversification of interests probably contributed partially to the slow development of the field as a profession. Even today, very few states have teacher certification specifically in TESOL. In any case, in an attempt to define the various groups and needs of the field, the Program Committee of the 1972 TESOL convention asked Betty Wallace Robinett to address this problem. Robinett defined the teaching of English as a continuum with the areas between the two extremes the proper domains of TESOL (84):

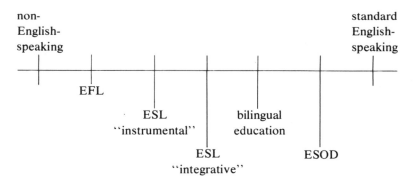

SOURCE: "The Domains of TESOL" by B.W. Robinett in *TESOL Quarterly* 6, no. 3 (1972): 192–207. Reprinted with permission.

English as a Foreign Language (EFL)

EFL refers to English as a Foreign Language "where English is looked upon as a cultural acquisition." Overseas where others study English the way persons in this country study French and Spanish, most teaching of

English is EFL. Although the early designation of this area was often EFL, publishers increasingly avoided the term, presumably because they considered the word *foreign* to be pejorative and hence to be avoided in the selling of textbooks. British usage in referring to overseas teaching is also EFL.

English as a Second Language (ESL)

ESL "instrumental" (the terms are Lambert's) refers to the learning of English for "specific functional purposes," i.e., self-serving such as for economic advantage; while "integrative" refers to interpersonal, assimilative purposes (56). In Robinett's terms, foreign students studying English in the United States for purposes of pursuing an American university degree would be ESL instrumental; others refer to it as EFL. The terminology is not as important as the underlying distinction which should be clarified.

Speaking from personal experience, for a Swede who by necessity learns English as the lingua franca of Europe, the experience is not very threatening. S/he has a perfectly good language and culture of her/his own, s/he considers her/himself fully equal to anything English or American, and more importantly, s/he expects this to be the mutual viewpoint. But consider the learning of English by such groups as the Navajo and the Chicano. The very fact that these children are pressured into accepting another culture and its medium of expression is likely to seem a derogatory comment on their own culture. When the contact between ethnic groups entails language learning for the subordinate group, the affective sphere of the process of second language learning is very different from foreign language learning, and the teacher can never afford to forget that. Minority group students have a great need for a sense of *dignidad de la persona,* the teacher's recognition of their rights as human beings. Tact can be more important than methods.

Bilingual Education (BE)

BE refers to programs where equal emphasis is placed on learning the native language as well as English. During the last decade BE has attracted the lion's share of federal funding for language teaching. The result has been occasional acrimony in job competition and shifting teacher competencies, and at times ESL programs have unfortunately been contrasted with BE programs as mutually exclusive. In what, to my mind, is an immoral position of "go hang the children but protect the teachers," the American Federation of Teachers has gone on record as opposing BE in the clear attempt to preserve jobs for its members (90,

92). It is therefore doubly important that readers have some knowledge of the development of BE in the United States and its relationship with ESL. The following may seem like a lengthy diversion, but it is important for an accurate understanding of the TESOL scene.

The end of the 1960s saw a trend to revive the identity of ethnic minorities, both at a cultural and a political level. The success of the Blacks when they showed a united front, the success of the bus strikes and the marches of the Civil Rights movement, were not lost upon the other ethnic minorities. The melting pot came to be regarded as a myth, and the new slogan was—and is—"from the melting pot to salad bowl." Schermerhorn (88) points out that ethnic groups that come into contact through annexation or colonization most often differ in goal orientation from groups that come into contact through voluntary migration. The Anglo superordinate group maintained its goal of assimilation for all, but the annexed Chicanos and the colonized Indians refused, preferring to maintain their cultural identity of which language is an integral part. Their goal is cultural pluralism with structural incorporation, i.e., access to goods and services and to social institutions like education and justice. In short, they want to retain their values and ways of life without being denied their fair share. This conflict is also mirrored in the educational sector. My own view is that controversial issues of bilingual education in the United States can best be understood as a part of a larger political movement which pits the subordinate ethnic minorities, rebelling against economic exploitation, in a power struggle with the dominant majority.

The actual situation is far more complicated than Schermerhorn's elegant framework allows for. It is a moot point how voluntary the migration is, if the alternative is a bloody revolution (as in the case of the escaped middle- and upper-class Cubans) or semi-starvation (as in the case of the illegal immigrants from Mexico). The Puerto Ricans migrate to New York and Chicago, but there is also considerable back-migration to Spanish-speaking Puerto Rico. Consequently many of the children know neither English nor Spanish well and feel ill at ease in both cultures. Puerto Ricans, unlike Mexican immigrants, are legal citizens of the United States. The major official language of Puerto Rico is Spanish, and many Puerto Ricans resent the situation in which as U.S. citizens they are denied the use of their official mother tongue on the continent. They also resent the transitional assimilation goals of bilingual education, and, indeed, the present programs in the United States are seen by the government officials as a more efficient way of teaching the national language where the tacit goal is language shift through bilingualism.

The earliest manner of dealing with the problem of instructing children in English which they did not understand was simply to ignore that problem. The children were put into regular classrooms with other

English-speaking children in a "sink-or-swim" situation; today such classes are sometimes referred to as "submersion" classes to distinguish them from the Canadian immersion programs.

The first advance in methodology and curriculum came from the field of ESL. It is probably accurate to say that ESL has never been given a fair chance in the public schools. The development of Fries's aural-oral method, intended for adults, came to contain primarily mechanical-type drills which the students could parrot without understanding a word.* These pattern drills were then used with school children instead of the modified language arts program they needed. Not surprisingly, the result was not encouraging. What is surprising is that the term ESL became identified in parts of the country with this particular method of teaching English as a second language, and ESL today remains rejected out of hand. Another reason for the lack of a fair chance is the insufficient number of teachers trained in methods of teaching English to children who don't know it; very few states require or recognize ESL teacher certification.

The present criticism of ESL by BE proponents is unfortunate for a number of reasons. ESL remains the only feasible alternative in schools which have students from a large number of different language backgrounds. Also, the consistent criticism of ESL as a pedagogical methodology (albeit for primarily political reasons) may serve to discredit the entire field of ESL; and, it must be remembered, a major component of a BE curriculum is exactly ESL. Without further advances in ESL methodology at the elementary level, BE may itself become discredited in the eyes of those who set national policy.

In 1968 the so-called Bilingual Education Act was approved. This Title VII amendment to the 1965 Elementary and Secondary Education Act provided the first federal funds for bilingual education "to meet the needs of children of limited English-speaking ability from low income families, so that these children will gain sufficient proficiency in English to keep up with their monolingual English-speaking peers in the educational system" (66). From the legislators' viewpoint, the programs are compensatory in nature; their objective is a more rapid and efficient acquisition of English. Such programs have become known as the transitional model.

The landmark case in bilingual education was *Lau* vs. *Nichols* in which a Chinese parent took the school board of San Francisco to court. "The plaintiffs claimed that the absence of programs designed to meet the linguistic needs of [non-English-speaking] children violated both Title VI and the Equal Protection Clause of the Fourteenth Amendment to the

---

*Certainly, this was never Fries's intention.

Constitution" (100). In 1974 the Supreme Court ruled unanimously in favor of *Lau*, avoiding the constitutional issue and relying solely on Title VI of the Civil Rights Act of 1964: "For students who do not understand English are effectively foreclosed from any meaningful education" (37). In other words, equal treatment does not constitute equal opportunity.

Subsequently, the Office of Civil Rights of the Department of Health, Education, and Welfare (HEW) appointed a task force to work out a set of guidelines for implementing the *Lau* decision, the so-called "*Lau* remedies," which have caused considerable furor. The constant excuse of school administrators who do not want to implement a bilingual education program in their schools is that the children do not need it as they have an ESL program. The "*Lau* remedies" therefore state again and again that an ESL program is not acceptable in a bilingual education program. Some people involved in ESL have misinterpreted this to mean that the children are not to be taught English. The "remedies" do end with a footnote stating that an ESL component is an integral part of a bilingual education program, and most certainly the task force never meant that the children were not to learn and be taught English.

The "*Lau* remedies" are implemented by the Lau Centers which serve under the Department of Education.* The federal government has indirect control over the states through the allocation of federal funding (total HEW expenditures on Bilingual Education and/or ESL projects for fiscal year 1980 amounted to nearly $150 million); and school districts judged out of compliance with the *Lau* decision stand the risk of losing all their federal funding, a powerful argument for the implementation of bilingual education and one not even the most conservative school board is willing to fight. Thus, slowly, through *Lau* violation rulings, litigation, and also through voluntary action at the state level, bilingual education programs are being implemented across the country. (The Massachusetts state legislature was the first to pass statutes mandating bilingual education, and its Massachusetts Transitional Bilingual Education Law of 1971 has served as a prototype for other states.) In many cases, however, it is clearly a legal-political process rather than the pragmatic-educational policy presumably intended by Congress in the transitional Bilingual Education Act of 1968.

The U.S. programs may legally be transitional in nature, but their major proponents, especially the ethnic group members involved in implementing the new directives, invariably refer to the programs as bilingual/bicultural and see the objectives as stable bilingualism with maintenance of the home culture as well as the home language. As the

---

*For a list of addresses of the Lau Centers, contact the Office of Bilingual Education and Minority Language Affairs, Department of Education, 400 Maryland Avenue, SW, Washington, DC 20202; (202) 245-2600.

NIE report points out, so far, "the Guidelines for the Title VII programs have been interpreted loosely enough" (66) to allow for maintenance programs as well as for transitional programs. In general, it is considered a crucial point in maintenance programs that teachers be members of the same ethnic group as the children, an ideological rather than a pedagogical consideration. I do not think the consequences of such policies on the children's English language acquisition have yet been dealt with.

Bilingual education changes the requirements of teacher competencies, and many programs are accompanied by chronic teacher strife as tenured Anglo teachers are fired in a job market without jobs in order to make room for bilingual teachers. Because of this confrontation of interest groups in competition for scarce jobs, it is not surprising that the discussion about pedagogical methodology sometimes takes the form of Bilingual Education *contra* ESL.

In fact, as long as one considers BE apart from its policy, it is immediately apparent that teaching English to minority children (inevitably ESL) is held by everyone to be an important function of BE programs. The standard and generally accepted U.S. Office of Education definition of BE (from the Title VII amendment to ESEA) calls for it:

> Bilingual education is the use of two languages, one of which is English, as mediums of instruction for the same pupil population in a well-organized program which encompasses part or all of the curriculum and includes the study of the history and culture associated with the mother tongue.

The form in which BE programs actually take shape in the classroom varies. Some classes have bilingual teachers who divide the school day between the L1 and the L2 in clearly separate units; others have bilingual teachers who use the so-called "concurrent translation" approach, alternating languages sentence by sentence. The latter approach may well be detrimental to learning, yet the method is widespread (58). Other classes function with an English-speaking teacher and an aide who is a native speaker of the children's L1. Such arrangements have been much criticized on the grounds that the children internalize the lower status of the aide vis à vis the teacher. The practice of course had its origin in expediency: no bilingual teachers were available. With continued implementation of BE, the teacher/aide arrangement is likely to be phased out; many aides are presently pursuing some form of teacher certification.

My own preference is for the Canadian model which separates the languages by teacher—a native-speaking English teacher and a native-speaking French teacher. Given the fact that very few people, and even fewer teachers, are perfectly bilingual, it solves the problem of teacher language proficiency.

Still other classes have only a monolingual English teacher in a regular program but are visited during the week by an ESL-trained teacher who takes some of the children in so-called "pull-out" classes, in which they work specifically on English language acquisition. Obviously, such programs do not deserve to be called bilingual, and they tend to be vehemently criticized by regular teachers, ESL teachers, and BE teachers alike. The regular teachers tend to dislike the commotion, the ESL teacher wants more time with the children, and the BE teacher wants the children taught in the mother tongue. However, in the not uncommon situation of some fifteen children from ten different language backgrounds at five different grade levels, it is understandable that the practice is resorted to. And if we listen to the children, it may not be totally reprehensible. At a recent conference in Toronto, eight tenth graders, who had immigrated to Canada four years earlier, insisted in the face of determined questioning that their first most helpful experience had been their pull-out ESL classes.

Unfortunately there is very little systematic knowledge of techniques and procedures for teaching children a second language at the elementary level which is coherently anchored in a theory of language acquisition. The elaboration of such a body of knowledge is an important priority for the future development of BE, because without it the entire approach of BE may fall into disillusion. And that would be a great pity because it is known that it is easier for non-English-speaking children to begin their schooling in BE programs.

To summarize, bilingual education in the United States today is a matter of federal law; the process of implementation reflects the sociopolitical situation. Slowly the children are coming to have an education which is an affirmation of their language and culture, an enormous task in a country as large and diverse as the United States. But it will be accomplished. Finally, the children themselves should have the last word on bilingual education: "Uno tiene mas opportunidad de aprender ingles sin necesidad de avergonzarse": One has a better opportunity to learn English and without the necessity to feel ashamed and make a fool of oneself (105).

English to Speakers of Other Dialects (ESOD)

The last domain of TESOL refers to ESOD, or more commonly today SESD (Standard English as a Second Dialect) which is the interest group for those who teach English to American Blacks whose home language is a distinct English dialect, variously called Non-Standard Negro English,

Afro-American English, but most commonly Black English. During the last ten years, Black English has been the focus of intense scholarly interest and work which are reflected in the teaching of Standard English (31). In the beginning there were attempts to adapt foreign language teaching techniques; but such methods, especially of the mechanical audiolingual variety, have not turned out very well, and most scholars today believe with Virginia Allen that "A Second Dialect Is Not a Foreign Language" (5). Some major issues have been (1) applying the linguistic descriptions of Black English to a study of interference in reading and writing and consequent implications for teaching (21); (2) an adequate history of Black English for teaching cultural pride and identity through understanding the legitimacy of Black English as a dialect in its own right (31); (3) the identification of speech acts, such as rapping, sounding, and jiving, and the legitimacy of Black culture (51); (4) language attitudes (91, 110); and (5) perhaps, above all, Labov's *The Study of Non-Standard English* (53).

Recently, there are clear trends indicating that SESD is becoming increasingly interested in nonstandard dialects, other than Black English, as, for example, in the issues surrounding the learning of standard English in Alaska by Native Americans, in the Caribbean, in Appalachia.

Altogether, the domains of TESOL range over a wide variety of situations and needs. Teachers need to take into account the particular situation of their students because the social, political, economic, and cultural factors tend to be of far more significance in influencing educational results than any language teaching methods per se.

WHO TEACHES WHAT TO WHOM FOR WHAT PURPOSE TO WHAT EFFECT

Who—the Teachers

Presumably because TESOL is so recently recognized as a profession in this country, it remains a fact that very few states require teachers to be certified in this area.* As a result, probably the majority of teachers who have nonnative English-speaking children in their classrooms have not been trained in TESOL. This is not to say that their teaching is necessarily bad—teaching is an art as much as, if not more than, a science, and good teachers learn more from their students than from any

---

*See Charles H. Blatchford, *Directory of Teacher Preparation Programs in TESOL and Bilingual Education 1978–1981* (Washington, D.C.: Teachers of English to Speakers of Other Languages, 1979).

training program. But good teachers also become frustrated when their classrooms become upset, their students don't learn, and they can't find answers to their very specific questions. Teaching ESOL is not just teaching but also content and subject matter and interaction with people who can be very different from the other students. This section attempts to deal with such problems, suggesting avenues to resources, sources for answers; in short, a survival manual for teachers.

What is the perfect ESL teacher like? Such a person doesn't exist of course except on paper. Even so, it is useful to consider possible characteristics in order to have a norm against which to measure one's own competencies and identify those areas most in need of improvement, whether knowledge, experience, understanding, or affect. I recommend the *Guidelines for the Certification and Preparation of Teachers of English to Speakers of Other Languages in the United States.* As the official guidelines of the professional organization TESOL, they reflect years of careful thought and discussion (101).

A source of help and information is the publisher of these guidelines, the professional organization TESOL (202 D.C. Transit Building, Georgetown University, Washington, DC 20057). Founded in 1966, TESOL serves a wide constituency of interests, as indicated by the following Special Interest Groups: (1) Teaching English Abroad; (2) English as a Foreign Language, for foreign students in English-speaking countries; (3) English as a Second Language, in elementary schools; (4) English as a Second Language, in secondary schools; (5) English as a Second Language, in higher education; (6) English as a Second Language, in bilingual education; (7) English as a Second Language, in adult education; (8) Standard English as a Second Dialect; and (9) Applied Linguistics (relevant linguistic studies and research). In addition, state and regional affiliates sponsor local conferences and workshops on a multitude of related issues. The inter/national organization has a publication program which addresses itself specifically to the needs of ESL teachers at all levels, as well as two regular publications, the *TESOL Quarterly* and the *TESOL Newsletter* (1a, 101a, 101b). I personally believe that every TESOL teacher will find it worthwhile to be a member of this professional organization.

Another source of information, the Center for Applied Linguistics (3520 Prospect Street, NW, Washington, DC 20007), has a publication program of interest to the ESL teacher, including the newsletter, *Linguistic Reporter;* and a staff of experts on topics ranging from textbooks and materials in ESL to literacy, BE, crosscultural awareness, and many others. Since 1975, CAL has run an information program, the National Indochinese Clearinghouse/Technical Assistance Center (toll-free, hotline telephone number: 800-424-3750) which gives practical advice on problems and issues related to the Vietnamese refugees. CAL also operates the ERIC Clearinghouse on Languages and Linguistics, one of the sixteen clearinghouses funded by the National Institute of Education.

A third source of information is the National Clearinghouse for Bilingual Education (1500 Wilson Boulevard, Suite 802, Rosslyn, VA 22209), with the free FORUM newsletter, a list of publications, and computer searches.

Another useful, and frequently overlooked, source of information is the foreign language teacher in the school or neighboring school, the teacher of Spanish, French, or German. There are more similarities between teaching ESL and teaching French than between teaching ESL and teaching English literature. Yet most often the English teachers become responsible for the ESL students, and it does not occur to anyone to ask colleagues in the foreign language teaching field for advice, even though they are an excellent source. And for the administrator who ponders to which teacher the responsibility for the ESL students should be assigned, I would like to add that our experience in the English Language Institute has been that a good teacher of Spanish or any other foreign language will become a good teacher of ESL with relatively little additional training.

Finally, there is the approach outlined in the following counsel: ESL teachers need the serenity to accept the things they cannot change, the courage to change the things they can, and the wisdom to know the difference.

What—the Subject

A useful distinction needs to be made in language teaching between linguistic competence and communicative competence; basically it is a distinction between form and social function of language. Linguistic competence refers to the speaker's knowledge of the language, the set or system of internalized rules about the language which enables her/him—to reject "he ate goldfish John" as un-English and to recognize that "flying planes can be dangerous" is ambiguous. Basically it refers to the grammar of the language.

Communicative competence, on the other hand, refers to the speaker's knowledge about the social rules of language use, to "the systemic sets of social interactional rules" (39), as well as to her/his linguistic competence. The argument is that it is not sufficient to teach simply the forms of the language but one must also teach the socially appropriate use of, in the present case, American English. This distinction is discussed in more detail in the following pages.

Linguistic Competence

What English should be taught? Because most teachers are likely to teach the English of their textbooks, texts become a very important matter in ESL and deserve careful consideration. The first step is to start an ESL textbook collection. The easiest way would be to convince the school librarian to undertake this task, but then each school will have its own policy on textbooks. Write the major publishers for lists of publications and also ask to be put on their mailing lists for announcements of new ESL texts. Most publishers will send examination copies which may either be returned or may be free. Try the university library. Write TESOL and the Center for Applied Linguistics and ask what bibliographies of textbooks they have available. Write CAL/ERIC. Call the chairperson of the ESL department of the local university and ask for suggestions. The point is that there exists a plethora of ESL texts, and only energy and a bit of individual ingenuity will provide access to them. It is worth the effort; good textbooks make life a lot easier.

The next step is choosing a text. It is a given that you really will not be able to tell whether it is a good text until you have tried it. And it is another given that no matter how good the text is, if you do not like it, for whatever reason, it will not work in your classroom. There is no absolute standard for textbooks; they always have to be evaluated in relationship to the teacher. Choose something you feel comfortable with.

As an example, in one of our workshops some teachers had a hard time evaluating a grammar text which employed a transformational-generative approach. The teachers were not familiar with T-G grammar. At that point it was irrelevant whether the text was good or bad because the teachers felt intimidated and uncomfortable with it.

Here are a few hints for consideration.

1. Be concerned primarily with the course objectives. (These are discussed in more detail in the "For What Purpose" section.)

2. Choose a text which is neither too easy nor too difficult. How can you tell? Without access to proficiency scores, the only honest answer is trial and error. If the text is too easy, the students will work very quickly, be bored and careless, and say that it is babyish work. But remember to ask them. If the text is too difficult, the students will not finish their work, they will be discouraged and say they will never learn English. They are more likely to blame themselves than the text. If students with different levels of proficiency are in the same class, they really should be working with different level texts, no matter how inconvenient for the teacher. In a pinch, I think students may be better judges of the difficulty level than the teacher. Ask their opinion. Also ask the salesperson or publisher. For reading materials, try the Cloze test; the technique is

discussed in Paulston and Bruder (72). Do not feel bad if you misjudged; it is very easy to do. Just be ready to change.

3. Check that the text provides a multiple of student activities. Good textbooks structure situations so that students learn. There should be opportunity for oral as well as written activities; but most importantly there should be communicative activities where students can exchange *new* information, talk about what *they* want to say, write about something important to *them*. Work through a set of exercises yourself and note your own reaction.

4. Check that the text contains grammar rules or explanations. Most students, except for young children, find such explanations helpful. They are also helpful for the teacher who is not trained in ESL. Most native speakers do not know the rules for the differences between, for example, *some* and *any,* or the present perfect and past tenses. It is very useful to have this information in the text. Also check the kind of rules: it is not enough to be told that the present perfect consists of the present of *have* plus the past participle/*-ed* as in *I have walked;* the difficulty lies in knowing when to *use* it. For those who have studied Spanish, just think about *ser* and *estar,* and you will understand this problem. The grammar explanations should be not only formal but also functional.

5. Be sure that the text emphasizes vocabulary and, of course, vocabulary which is useful to the students. If vocabulary is salient, it is easy to learn; if it is not, it is a drag. One probably learns grammar and guesses at the meaning of grammar to a large extent from the semantic relationship of lexical items. Given *bite, dog,* and *mailman,* everyone thinks of a dog biting a mailman; for this reason "dog was bitten by mailman" makes the headlines and the passive is a difficult pattern to learn. One of the weaknesses of the audiolingual method was its neglect of vocabulary, and traces of that neglect still linger. Make sure the text emphasizes vocabulary learning.

6. Make sure the content is interesting to students. Urban students do not much care to read exclusively about the rural United States and vice versa. Do *not* use elementary school texts with large print for high school students even if the language is at their level. Avoid texts with dated pictures; high school students have very little tolerance for what is not *now*.

Finally, if the students like it and you like it and it works, i.e., the students learn from it, then don't worry about whether it is a good text or not. Kenneth Pike used to say that classroom teachers know what it will take linguists another ten years to discover. Never mind that you can't explain why it works, it is quite sufficient for you to know that it does.

Besides worrying about textbooks, the teacher needs at least two additional resources: a reference grammar or two and a good dictionary.

Quirk and Greenbaum's *Concise Grammar of Contemporary English* is one I like, extensive and rather technical (78). Crowell's *Index to Modern English* remains my own favorite throughout the years; it is an index of all the patterns that Crowell's students consistently made errors on, and it gives rules in simple and clear English—it can also be used by advanced students (27). As for dictionaries, my own preference for ESL purposes is the Heritage Dictionary. For reasons I have never understood, some teachers won't allow their students to use bilingual dictionaries. Try to look up the definition of a word you don't know where you can't understand the definition and see how helpful it is. As long as students find bilingual dictionaries useful, let them use them. They won't much care to be thought different from the rest, and they will stop using them as soon as they can.

Communicative Competence

Generally, communicative competence is taken to be the objective of language teaching: the production of speakers competent to communicate in the target language. Divergent opinions arise, however, when one tries to isolate the skills needed for efficient communication. Language teachers tend to equate communicative competence with the ability to carry out linguistic interaction in the target language. But efficient communication requires also that speakers share the social meaning of the linguistic forms, that they have the same social rules for language use (33, 39, 41, 43). Dell Hymes, the anthropologist, argues that communicative competence must include not only the linguistic forms of a language but also a knowledge of when, how, and to whom it is appropriate to use these forms (45, 46). All teachers teach the *wh*-questions early in the curriculum, but they don't teach the questions one can and cannot ask. If you were to ask me how much money I make, I would probably consider you drunk, somewhat mad, or very rude. Yet in some countries, this is a highly polite question. The social meaning of the same linguistic form varies from culture to culture. Communication includes nonverbal behavior as well. As often cited, eye contact behavior carries the meaning of honest dealings in Anglo culture while it is rude and disrespectful in Hispanic and in many other cultures. This is probably well known, but how many teachers have taught "proper" eye contact behavior to students? Obviously there is nothing inherently more proper about one set of behaviors vis-à-vis another except in cultural appropriateness. On a superficial level, communicative competence may simply be defined as tact and good manners, and people not sharing that system will consider others rude and tactless. Teachers do their students a disservice if they don't teach them the social rules along with the linguistic rules as long as they remember not to imply any moral superiority of one rule over the other.

Occasionally, faulty rule sharing will lead to complete breakdown in communication. Here is an example from a recent stay in Sweden, where I was born and raised. We (my American husband and children) celebrated Thanksgiving by having my immediate family (Swedish) and friends for a traditional turkey dinner. I was busy in the kitchen and came belatedly into the living room where my sister-in-law had just arrived. In impeccable Swedish I ask her politely, "Do you know everyone?" Any native American would correctly interpret such a question to mean that I wanted to know if she had been introduced to those guests she had not previously met. She looked at me sourly and said, "I don't know everyone, but if you are asking me if I have greeted everyone, I have." Fussed as I was, and in such an archetypical American situation, I had momentarily forgotten that proper manners demand that Swedes do not wait to be introduced by a third party, but go around the room, shake hands with everyone, and say their name aloud to those they have not previously met. Because any child knows that, my sister-in-law felt I had reprimanded her for bad manners, for faulty sharing of a systemic set of social interactional rules. Clearly, the meaning of an interaction is easily misinterpreted if the speakers don't share the same set of rules. Hence the necessity for teaching those rules.

This anecdote also illustrates another aspect of communicative competence: it is easier to keep one's linguistic codes separate than one's social codes as one is often not aware of the social codes on a conscious level until they are violated. It is much easier to be bilingual than bicultural.

Several books discuss techniques for teaching communicative competence and many linguists think this is an important and necessary supplement to the regular curriculum (17, 40, 72, 74, 81). But there is one matter which I want to stress strongly. People have very deep-seated beliefs that their competence rules are the only real, valid ones, and this tendency needs to be watched. It is not rude to correct a student whose behavior one reacts to as deviant as long as it is done tactfully. The important thing to remember is not to imply any moral superiority of one rule over another, to remember the difference between adding rules and substituting rules. In the latter case, one obviously rejects the value of the first set of rules and rejects the very culture of the student. Thus the emphasis should be on *teaching* communicative competence, not on correcting forms which deviate from it.

I may not particularly like eating a meal with my fingers, but at least I know better than to use my left hand if I am served a Moroccan dinner. One does not have to like others' cultural rules to find a relief from anxiety and an ease of communication in knowing what those rules are.

For many students the teacher will be the most important cultural broker, the most important source of information (where can one find rules for eye contact written down?) for all these strange new ways of doing things. This is a responsibility for the ESL teacher to take seriously.

Whom—the Students

The other side of the coin of teaching students the communicative competence rules of the mainstream is for teachers to learn about the culture of their students, to learn something about crosscultural communication. I offer the following eleven do's and don'ts (of which I think the last is the most important) for teachers who have students from other cultures or subcultures.

1. Do understand that there is no such thing as a culturally deprived child (by culture is meant the consistent value systems and beliefs held by a group or simply that group's unified way of looking at the world). There are culturally different children, yes, but they have a perfectly good culture of their own which in all likelihood they prefer to that of the mainstream. Even though the objective of many public schools is the socialization of children into mainstream cultural values—and, remember, no one may favor this more than the parents—socialization need not entail the denial of their own culture, so often accompanied by self-hate.

2. Do understand that the language these children speak—or dialect, and this is as true of lower-class Whites as of lower-class Blacks—is as perfectly good a linguistic system as the teacher's standard English; it is just different. To deny that *ain't* is a word or to claim that "I ain't got no book" really means that you have got a book because two negatives make a positive is not only silly but also linguistically incorrect. This does not mean that you should not teach standard English, only that you should do so without disparaging the child's mother tongue. After all, students learned their way of talking at home, and by making clear you don't like it, what you are really telling them is what you think of their family. And children are more perceptive than you may realize; they will understand your criticism of their family background long before it dawns on you what you are doing. Do be careful of comments on students' speech; language is an integral part of their sense of self and ego-identity.

3. Do recognize that different cultures may share the same moral values but express them differently on the surface. To look someone straight in the eye may signal honesty and aboveboard dealings to a mainstream teacher, but Hispanic children have often been carefully taught to avoid direct eye contact in order to show respect. An American

Indian child will show respect by speaking softly, and the loudness of voice which satisfies the teacher is a clear sign of anger to that child. Because few teachers have been exposed to a contrastive cultural etiquette, it might be well to take a look at some of the entries in the bibliography, especially Burger and Abrahams-Troike (1, 17, 20, 42, 51, 87, 94, 110).

4. Don't be a Puritan ethnic with these children. Different cultures use different strategies for sanctions and rewards, and to plug someone into the wrong system just doesn't work. Internalized guilt—the touchstone of the Puritan ethic—doesn't work in a cultural system where shame is the controlling sanction. Middle-class Anglo children have internalized a set of sanctions and will self-monitor their behavior, the "you-can-trust-them-to-be-good" sort of thing. Other cultures such as Hispanic, Arab, and ghetto Black monitor behavior with external sanctions. Shame is external, and appeal to someone's nonexistent guilt feelings is just more tuned-out teacher talk. Teachers are so constantly admonished never to use sarcasm in the classroom that they never resort to it except when angry, and then it is indeed resented by mainstream children. But in cultures where shame is a controlling sanction, verbal ridicule is a very powerful force. Many a toughie in the classroom, whose very toughness is enhanced by an unflinching attitude to the teacher's scolding, would mind very much being made to lose face. Sarcasm is not good because it indicates inherent animosity and lack of good will, but if you can think of a loving kind of sarcasm, sarcasm with good will, you will find it more efficient for directing behavior than moral lectures. One of my staff reports the following incident: "On the fourth day of class, two Latin American students were ten minutes late. It was reported by the others that they had gone for coffee. When they came in, I commented, 'I hope the coffee was good,' much to the amusement of the others. No one has been late since."

5. Do be consistent and explicit in your own behavior. Most of the ESL students come from authoritarian homes and you do them no favor with a permissive attitude. They will take advantage of it, and also lose respect for you. Remember, these children are not culturally deprived but they are culturally different. It is very difficult (as well as tiring) to figure out what motivates specific behaviors of people in another culture, which is why it is so important that teachers be consistent in their behavior and that they clearly outline their specific rules. Since the particular configuration of values on which these rules are based may not necessarily be shared by all students, teachers should therefore take care to explain them. Most of all, remember that a bleeding heart attitude does these children no good at all. Make certain they are held to the same exacting standards as other students. Teacher expectation of pupil work

is crucial in determining the quality of the work students produce. It is merely inverted discrimination to expect less and to let ESL students get by with less than acceptable work.

6. Do reassess your ways of interacting with students. It is typical of most of the cultures discussed here that people tend to relate to persons, not to abstract moral values. For example, there is no way that I can convince some of my students to come on time by appealing to the moral value (which they don't share) of punctuality. But they will come on time if I explain that I feel it an insult to my worth as a teacher when they are late; and if they want to express their respect for me personally (not as a teacher), they will come on time. This kind of strategy is repugnant to many mainstream teachers, but it does work since these children have been socialized initially in this manner.

7. Do reevaluate kinds of assignments. In many cultures there is a certain degree of fatalism, of *mañanaism,* and a concordant lack of personal responsibility. Certainly try to encourage the growth of such responsibility, but also recognize that other cultures do not do so to the same degree. Nobody likes to do homework, but when both the physical conditions of the home (such as large families with no possibilities for privacy, etc.) and the cultural attitudes toward unsupervised work dictate against its being done, then out-of-class assignments become counterproductive. Since most students have enough study halls to finish their work if it is supervised, take the trouble to talk to the study hall teachers of students who have difficulties in doing their homework. Or have students do it in your own class. Or whatever else you can think of. But do not just condemn the children for being lazy and let them slide so far behind they will never catch up.

8. Do give recognition in class of the value of the other culture. It is not enough just to voice it; an active demonstration of your respect is also necessary. A brief language lesson each week with students acting as teacher works very well. Invite parents or adults to come in and discuss their occupations, and remember that everybody does not want to become middle class. It may be difficult for teachers to understand that a little boy's ambition may well be to become a garbage collector like his father, but the garbage collector may have equal difficulty understanding why anyone would want to become a teacher. There is no need therefore to present only professional occupations; there is a need to present successful role models (in whatever occupation) from minority groups. You may, however, want to present a woman doctor or lawyer; professional women are also a minority group. Certainly you can think of many such activities yourself, keeping in mind that one of the most important things to teach the Anglo children is a genuine interest in and respect for other cultures.

9. Do be alert to the possibility of contextual constraints in the teaching situation. Burger tells the anecdote of a program of prenatal care for lower-class girls in Chile (17). Offered in the local school, it was a complete flop. It so happened that in Chile sitting in a classroom was associated with childish status, but social clubs were very much in and desired upper-class behavior. When the meetings were held instead in a private home with refreshments served, the program became a huge success.

Peer teaching may be a viable alternative when the teacher cannot get through to the student. Be careful with male-female relationships in pairing students for team work. Don't punish children for speaking their own language. But most of all be alert to the fact that another culture may place an interpretation very different from yours on the same phenomenon.

10. The foregoing suggestions don't mean that you will not have individual aberrations, but they are difficult to spot in another culture with which you are not familiar. Don't just write off outrageous behavior as typical of X culture. Do as the anthropologists do and work with informants from the same culture in order to find out as much as possible about specific sets of behavior which you find disturbing.

11. And, finally, do take with a grain of salt all the good advice experts pour over you. Sincere liking and respect for all your students is still the prerequisite of all good teaching. All the good advice in the world cannot give you that if you don't have it; and if you have it, you can move the earth. Don't underestimate the tremendous importance a teacher can have in the lives of individual students.

For What Purpose—Objectives

It is not profound to say that the objectives and needs of students should be the overriding consideration for all decisions—it is merely common sense. The basic objective for ESL students in the public schools is perfectly clear: to be able to follow everyday instruction in English. The ESL program is a temporary support program. There is no reason why ESL students should not follow the regular program in music, physical education, industrial arts, home economics, and such classes from the very first day. This is a good place to emphasize that ESL students belong in the classes of their age group. The best language teachers are the students' English-speaking classmates; non-English-speaking students should *not* be placed in lower grades because of their lack of proficiency in English.

As much as possible, the regular assignments and activities should be incorporated into the ESL curriculum. For beginning students this is very difficult, but with ingenuity it can be done. It need be nothing involved. If the student is taking chorus, for example, help him/her work on pronunciation of the lyrics. Find a student who knows his/her language to help translate. Work on the vocabulary in the directions for home economics and use a lot of peer teaching and translation. Each teacher can think of many more such activities. What is important is that the student feel part of the society of the whole school, seeing English as a tool for getting things done, and in fact getting things done from the very beginning. ESL should not be a ghetto.

It goes without saying that textbooks should be selected to meet the students' scholastic needs, from vocabulary to activities such as writing book reports, taking tests, filling in study hall passes, and all the other language functions of school life.

But students also live in the real world. Find out what their other needs are. Filling out medical records at the doctor's office? Applying for a driver's license? Opening a bank account? Getting a job? Whatever the student needs, the more the ESL classroom work can meet them, the more effective the learning. Bring in forms and work on filling them out; role play job interviews; take students to the bank. Home visits may be a thing of the past, but try them. You may be the cultural broker for the student, but many students in turn are the main cultural brokers for their mothers. Find out the mother's needs, the family's needs. Granted this is time-consuming and difficult, but it can also be very rewarding.

For many ESL students, their ESL teacher becomes their major resource person in those difficult early days. Be aware of that need. And in case you think it is not your job, remember that your students will learn as much English from such exchanges as anything you can teach them from a textbook.

To What Effect—Methods and Techniques

How effectively do we teach ESL? Most teachers will look to methods and techniques for the answer to that question. This section briefly discusses various methods and refers the reader to additional sources of information.

The audiolingual method, pure behaviorist theory, and Moulton's five slogans are gone from the ESL scene. A variety of methods (many of which I think are the emperor's new clothes all over but which many people like) hold the stage. Perhaps the best way to introduce this section is to give Prator's ten slogans (which he suggested to replace Moulton's five):

1. Teaching is more of an art than a science.
2. No methodologist has the whole answer.

3. Try to avoid the pendulum syndrome.
4. Place a high value on practical experimentation without doctrinaire allegiance.
5. Look to various relevant disciplines for insights.
6. View objectives as overriding considerations.
7. Regard all tested techniques as resources.
8. Attach as much importance to what your students say as to how they say it.
9. Let your greatest concern be the needs and motivation of your students.
10. Remember that what is new is not necessarily better.* (76)

Described by Prator as an attitude toward teaching, these slogans express very well the commonsensical approach advocated throughout this book.

In 1969 Wardhaugh predicted that cognitive psychology would influence language teaching for many years to come and thus far his prediction holds (106). Ausubel (8) is still frequently cited in footnotes, everyone insists that language learning must be meaningful, no one claims that language learning is a straightforward matter of habit formation, and there seems to be a general consensus that grammatical rules and explanations are beneficial for adults. Carroll sums up the implications of the present tenets of psychology for language teaching in his excellent article "Learning Theory for the Classroom Teacher," emphasizing a commonsense approach which includes a knowledge of objectives, individualized learning, and high-quality instruction (18).

Besides cognitive psychology, psycholinguistics (23, 30) and neurolinguistics (2, 59, 60) are areas of study receiving a lot of attention. Especially in regard to neurolinguistics, caution is needed in drawing implications for the classroom. At this point I think it is safe to say that the evidence (from aphasia, split brain operations, dichotic listening tests, etc.) indicates that individuals have different ways of learning for which there may be a biological foundation. But that was known before. I find the readings in neurolinguistics the most interesting in the language learning field today. But I worry about premature applications, and I react against the fads which claim to draw on neurolinguistics.

In psycholinguistics there has been a spate of so-called second language (L2) acquisition research. There, too, it is still early to predict the implications; any premature recommendations for specific techniques should be taken with a grain of salt. It is difficult to single out specific studies. The issues of the last four years of *Language Learning* and the proceedings of 1975's Georgetown Round Table (30) are a good introduc-

---

*"In Search of a Method" by C. Prator, in *Readings on English as a Second Language*, edited by Kenneth Croft, published 1980 by Winthrop Publishers, Inc., Cambridge, Mass. Reprinted by permission.

tion, but the best place to begin is probably Roger Brown's *A First Language* (15). His basic finding is that "there is an approximately invariant order to acquisition for the 14 morphemes we have studied, and behind this invariance lies not modeling frequency but semantic and grammatical complexity" (15). Furthermore, he posits the concept of semantic saliency, a notion which may hold direct implications for language teaching.

After this brief detour of present-day influences on ESL, a specific look at methods should be helpful. The audiolingual method has been totally discredited, maybe at times unfairly, as it is blamed for infelicities which Fries certainly never intended. A careful reading of his *Teaching and Learning English as a Foreign Language* will reveal it as sensible a book today as the day it was written (35). Cognitive code (John Carroll's term) is generally recognized to be the major new trend, with its emphasis on meaningful learning and careful analysis of linguistic structures. The cognitive code approach can be considered a reaction against the audiolingual, both from theoretical and practical viewpoints. An excellent and detailed account of this approach can be found in Chastain, *Developing Second-Language Skills: Theory to Practice* (22). The approach closely reflects the transformational-generative linguistic school of thought about the nature of language, and it is influenced by cognitive psychologists, critical of stimulus-reinforcement theory, such as Ausubel (8). It holds that language is a rule-governed creative system of a universal nature. Language learning must be meaningful, rote-learning should be avoided, and the primary emphasis is on analysis and developing competence in Chomsky's sense of the word (see the definition of linguistic competence on page 19). There is the same nice fit between linguistic theory and psychological theory in cognitive code methodology as there once was in the audiolingual method. The trouble with cognitive code is that I know of not one single textbook for beginning students which can be classified as strict cognitive code.

In practice, most language teaching specialists are eclectic, as are the textbooks they write. Carroll holds that there is nothing mutually exclusive in the theories of Skinner and of Lenneberg-Chomsky about language learning but rather that these theories are complementary (19). This opinion is reflected in the eclectic approach to methodology characteristic of all the best methods texts at the technique level, what Chastain calls "cookbooks." The following is my own list of practical, down-to-earth, methods texts, most of which are written by people who have themselves been language teachers:

1. Allen, Edward D., and Valette, Rebecca M. *Classroom Techniques: Foreign Languages and English as a Second Language.* New York: Harcourt Brace Jovanovich, 1977.

2. Chastain, Kenneth. *Developing Second-Language Skills: Theory to Practice.* 2d ed. Chicago: Rand, McNally, 1976.
3. Dacanay, Fe R. *Techniques and Procedures in Second-Language Teaching.* Quezon City: Phoenix Press, 1963.
4. Dubin, Fraida, and Olshtain, Elite. *Facilitating Language Learning: A Guidebook for the ESL/EFL Teacher.* New York: McGraw-Hill, 1977.
5. Finocchiaro, Mary. *English as a Second Language: From Theory to Practice.* New York: Regents, 1974.
6. Fries, Charles C. *Teaching and Learning English as a Foreign Language.* Ann Arbor: University of Michigan Press, 1945.
7. Ilyin, Donna, and Tragardh, Thomas, eds. *Classroom Practices in Adult ESL.* Washington, D.C.: TESOL, 1978.
8. Paulston, C. B., and Bruder, M. N. *From Substitution to Substance: A Handbook of Structural Pattern Drills.* Rowley, Mass.: Newbury House, 1975.
9. Paulston, C. B., and Bruder, M. N. *Teaching English as a Second Language: Techniques and Procedures.* Cambridge, Mass.: Winthrop, 1976.
10. Rivers, Wilga M., and Temperly, Mary S. *A Practical Guide to the Teaching of English as a Second or Foreign Language.* New York: Oxford University Press, 1978.
11. Rivers, Wilga M. *Speaking in Many Tongues: Essays in Foreign Language Teaching.* 2d ed. Rowley, Mass.: Newbury House, 1976.
12. Rivers, Wilga M. *Teaching Foreign-Language Skills.* Chicago: University of Chicago Press, 1968.
13. Robinett, Betty W. *Teaching English to Speakers of Other Languages: Substance and Technique.* New York: McGraw-Hill, 1978.
14. Saville-Troike, Muriel. *Foundations for Teaching English as a Second Language: Theory and Method for Multicultural Education.* Englewood Cliffs, N.J.; Prentice-Hall, 1976.
15. Stevick, E. W. *Adapting and Writing Language Lessons.* Washington, D.C.: Foreign Service Institute, 1976.
16. Stevick, E. W. *Teaching Languages: A Way and Ways.* Rowley, Mass.: Newbury House, 1980.

Most of these writers agree that all four skills—listening, speaking, reading, and writing—should be introduced simultaneously without undue postponement of any one. The importance of writing as a service activity for the other skills is generally recognized and there is considerable interest in controlled composition. No one talks any longer about memorizing long dialogues. Listening comprehension is still poorly understood on a theoretical level, but there is more emphasis on the teaching of that skill. The crucial importance of vocabulary, the ignoring of which was one of the worst faults of the audiolingual approach, is increasingly gaining acceptance.

There is probably agreement with Chastain that "perhaps too much attention has been given to proper pronunciation" (22), and there is now a tendency to think it is more important for the learner to communicate ideas than to practice utterances with perfect pronunciation. The one thing that everyone is absolutely certain about is the necessity to use language for communicative purposes in the classroom. As early as 1968 Oller and Obrecht concluded from an experiment that communicative activity should be a central point of pattern drills from the very first stages of language learning (70). Savignon's widely cited dissertation in 1971 confirmed that beyond doubt (86). There is some bridling at pattern drills, but, more importantly, there is agreement on the basic principle of meaningful learning for the purpose of communication. And that basic principle is indicative of what may be the most significant trend: increasing concentration on student learning rather than on teaching (69).

In addition to the prevailing eclecticism, several new methods have gained visibility recently in the United States. In alphabetical order they are as follows: Community Counseling-Learning, Notional-Functional Syllabus, Rapid Acquisition, the Silent Way, Suggestopedia, and Total Physical Response. The Monitor Model (52) should perhaps be mentioned here, too; but at this point it is a theoretical model of language learning rather than a method for language teaching.

Community Counseling-Learning or Community Language Learning (CLL) was developed by Charles A. Curran (28) from his earlier work in affective psychology. In CLL the students sit in a circle with a tape recorder and talk about whatever interests them. The teacher, whose role is seen as a counselor, serves as a resource person rather than as a traditional "teacher." At the very beginning stages, the counselor also serves as translator for the clients: students first utter in their native language, the teacher translates, and students repeat their own utterances in the L2. The tape is played back, errors analyzed, and clients copy down whatever structures they need to work on. Adherents of this method tend to be ardent in their fervor, pointing out that it teaches "the whole person" within a supportive community which minimizes the risk-taking held necessary for language learning. Another value of this method lies in the motivational aspect in that students can talk about issues of concern to them (28, 96, 97).

The Notional-Functional Syllabus was developed in Europe and is best known through Wilkins's *Notional Syllabuses* (104, 109). ("Syllabus" here means textbook content.) Basically, this approach sees the organizing factor for a syllabus or curriculum to be functional aspects of language rather than formal. Instead of taking an inventory (which is incomplete anyway, says Wilkins) of grammar patterns and arranging the textbook after them, one takes categories of communicative function, like judgment and evaluation, suasion, argument, rational inquiry and exposition, personal emotions and emotional relations, and then arranges the grammar patterns wherever they turn up in these categories. Wilkins's concern is primarily with communicative competence:

> In drawing up a notional syllabus, instead of asking how speakers of the language express themselves or when and where they use the language, we ask what it is they communicate through language. We are then able to organize language teaching in terms of the content rather than the form of the language. (109)

He also insists on a linguistic, formal component in the curriculum, but that insistence occasionally gets lost in the enthusiasm of his followers in the United States.

Rapid Acquisition of a Foreign Language by Avoidance of Speaking is an approach developed by Winitz and Reeds (111). The authors believe that there is a natural sequence (neurological) in language learning and stress listening comprehension until it is complete before students are allowed to speak. Length of utterance is limited, problem solving through the use of pictures is stressed, and the syllabus is limited to base structures and limited vocabulary.

The Silent Way was developed by Caleb Gattegno in 1963 but not published here until 1972. In this method, the teacher uses Cuisinière rods, a color-coded wall chart for pronunciation, and speaks each new word only *once;* the responsibility for learning and talking is shifted to the students. Even correction is handled through gestures and mime by the teacher with no further modeling. Many teachers are enthused by this method, but there are also anecdotes of student rebellion (36, 96).

Suggestopedia, a method developed by Georgi Lozanov at the Institute of Suggestology in Sofia, Bulgaria (9, 62), claims to reduce the strain of language learning. Listening and speaking are stressed with emphasis on vocabulary acquisition. The Suggestopedic Cycle begins with review of previously learned material in the target language, followed by introduction of new material. This is followed by a one-hour séance during which students listen to the new material against a background of baroque music. The students also do breathing exercises and yoga relaxation techniques which are said to increase concentration and tap the powers of the subconscious. There is also considerable role play of real-life situations.

Total Physical Response, developed by James Asher (6, 7), also stresses listening comprehension, as he believes that if listening and speaking are introduced simultaneously, listening comprehension is much delayed. Basically the method consists of having students listen to commands and then carrying them out.

I refrain from commenting on these methods since the opinion that is important is the teacher's. As long as teacher *and students* have confidence that they are in fact learning, and all are happy in the process, I don't think the methods make too much difference.

CONCLUSION

I would like to conclude by acknowledging that a classroom teacher's job is one of the most taxing in the world. Not only must the teacher be knowledgeable about her/his subject and prepared for classes, but the sheer psychic energy needed to deal with lively children and adolescents all day long is rarely recognized except by other classroom teachers. The task of the teacher in schools whose students include children from other cultures is doubly difficult. Furthermore, when in addition those cultures represent minority groups with a long tradition of social and economic exploitation by white middle-class Anglos, the classroom situation often becomes unbearably difficult. Often these children are held to be slow to learn, they do not read at the expected national levels, they are late, they do not do their homework, they are quiet and noisy and hostile, and so on. Often these allegations are true; and when the children do not learn, the teacher is blamed. The teacher thus becomes the public scapegoat for all the social ills, for the problems of the schools reflect the problems and social injustices of the larger society which are totally beyond the control of an individual classroom teacher. Nevertheless, in spite of these difficulties, the enormous influence a good teacher can have on the life of an individual student is not sufficiently emphasized. Teachers who care passionately that their students learn English will have students who care, too. And it should not be forgotten that without English these students will never have a chance for full participation in the life of this country. The extent of the teacher's responsibilities is awesome.

SELECTED REFERENCES

1. Abrahams, R., and Troike, R. *Language and Culture Diversity in American Education.* Englewood Cliffs, N.J.: Prentice-Hall, 1972.
1a. Alatis, James E. "TESOL: Teaching English to Speakers of Other Languages." In *Learning a Second Language.* 79th Yearbook of the National Society for the Study of Education. Chicago: University of Chicago Press, 1980.
2. Albert, M. L., and Obler, L. K., *The Bilingual Brain: Neuropsychological and Neurolinguistic Aspects of Bilingualism.* New York: Academic Press, 1978.
3. Allen, E. D., and Valette, R. M. *Classroom Techniques: Foreign Languages and English as a Second Language.* New York: Harcourt Brace Jovanovich, 1977.
4. Allen, H. B., and Campbell, R. N., eds. *Teaching English as a Second Language: A Book of Readings.* New York: McGraw-Hill, 1972.
5. Allen, V. F. "A Second Dialect Is Not a Foreign Language." In *Linguistics and the Teaching of Standard English to Speakers of Other Languages,* edited by J. Alatis. Washington, D.C.: Georgetown University Press, 1969.
6. Asher, J. J., and Adamski, C. *Learning Another Language Through Actions: The Complete Teacher's Guidebook.* Los Gatos, Calif.: Sky Oak Productions, 1977.
7. Asher, J. "The Total Physical Response Approach to Second Language Learning." *Modern Language Learning* 53, no. 1 (1969): 3–17.
8. Ausubel, D. P. *Educational Psychology: A Cognitive View.* New York: Holt, Rinehart, and Winston, 1968.
9. Bancroft, W. J. "The Lozanov Method and Its American Adaptations." *Modern Language Journal* 62, no. 4 (1978): 167–74.
10. Bloomfield, L. *Language.* New York: Holt, Rinehart and Winston, 1933.
11. Boas, F. *Introduction to the Handbook of American Indian Languages.* Washington, D.C.: Georgetown University Press, 1963.
12. Bowen, D. *Patterns of English Pronunciation.* Rowley, Mass.: Newbury House, 1975.
13. _____. "The Structure of Language." In *Linguistics in School Programs,* edited by A. Marckwardt. 69th Yearbook of the National Society for the Study of Education. Chicago: University of Chicago Press, 1970.
14. Brooks, N. *Language and Language Learning: Theory and Practice.* 2d ed. New York: Harcourt Brace Jovanovich, 1964.
15. Brown, R. *A First Language: The Early Stages.* Cambridge, Mass.: Harvard University Press, 1973.
16. Bumpass, F. L. *Teaching Young Students English as a Foreign Language.* New York: American Book, 1963.
17. Burger, H. *Ethno-Pedagogy: Cross-Cultural Teaching Techniques.* Albuquerque, N.M.: Southwestern Cooperative Educational Laboratory, 1971.

18. Carroll, J. "Learning Theory for the Classroom Teacher." In *The Challenge of Communication,* edited by G. A. Jarvis, pp. 142–45. Skokie, Ill.: National Textbook Company, 1974.
19. _____. "Current Issues in Psycholinguistics and Second Language Teaching." *TESOL Quarterly* 5, no. 2 (1971): 101–14.
20. Cazden, C. B.; John, V. P.; and Hymes, D., eds. *Functions of Language in the Classroom.* New York: Teachers College Press, 1972.
21. Center for Applied Linguistics. *Urban Language Series.* Arlington, Va.
22. Chastain, K. *Developing Second-Language Skills: Theory to Practice.* 2d ed. Chicago: Rand, McNally, 1976.
23. Clark, H. E., and Clark, E. V. *Psychology and Language.* New York: Harcourt Brace Jovanovich, 1977.
24. Corder, S. P., and Allen, J. P. B. *The Edinburgh Course in Applied Linguistics, Vol. 2, Papers in Applied Linguistics.* London: Oxford University Press, 1974.
25. _____. *The Edinburgh Course in Applied Linguistics, Vol. 3, Techniques in Applied Linguistics.* London: Oxford University Press, 1974.
26. Croft, K., ed. *Readings on English as a Second Language.* Cambridge, Mass.: Winthrop, 1980.
27. Crowell, T. L. *Index to Modern English.* New York: McGraw-Hill, 1964.
28. Curran, C. A. *Counseling-Learning in Second Languages.* Apple River, Ill.: Apple River Press, 1976.
29. Dacanay, F. R. *Techniques and Procedures in Second-Language Teaching.* Quezon City: Phoenix Press, 1963. Reprinted and distributed by Oceana Press, Dobbs Ferry, N.Y.
30. Dato, D., ed. *Developmental Psycholinguistics: Theory and Applications.* Georgetown University Round Table on Languages and Linguistics. Washington, D.C.: Georgetown University Press, 1975.
31. Dillard, J. L. *Black English: Its History and Usage in the United States.* New York: Vintage Books, 1972.
32. Diller, K. *The Language Teaching Controversy,* Rowley, Mass.: Newbury House, 1978.
33. Ervin-Tripp, S. *Language Acquisition and Communicative Choice.* Stanford, Calif.: Stanford University, 1973.
34. Finocchiaro, M. *English as a Second Language: From Theory to Practice.* New York: Regents, 1974.
35. Fries, C. C. *Teaching and Learning English as a Foreign Language.* Ann Arbor: University of Michigan Press, 1945.
36. Gattegno, C. *Teaching Foreign Languages in Schools the Silent Way.* 2d ed. New York: Educational Solutions, 1972.
37. Geffert, H. et al. *The Current Status of U.S. Bilingual Education Legislation.* Arlington, Va.: Center for Applied Linguistics, 1975.
38. Gleason, H. A., Jr. *An Introduction to Descriptive Linguistics.* New York: Holt, Rinehart and Winston, 1955.
39. Grimshaw, A. D. "Rules, Social Interaction, and Language Behavior." *TESOL Quarterly* 7, no. 2 (June 1972): 99–115.
40. *Guidelines for Communication Activities.* Singapore: RELC, 1979.
41. Gumperz, J. *Language in Social Groups.* Stanford, Calif.: Stanford University, 1971.

42. Hall, E. *The Silent Language.* New York: Doubleday, 1959.
43. Hannerz, U. "The Second Language: An Anthropological View." *TESOL Quarterly* 7, no. 3 (September 1973): 235–48.
44. Harris, D. *Testing English as a Second Language.* New York: McGraw-Hill, 1969.
45. Hymes, D. "Models of the Interaction of Language and Social Life." In *Directions in Sociolinguistics,* edited by John Gumperz and Dell Hymes. New York: Holt, Rinehart and Winston, 1972.
46. _____. "The Anthropology of Communication." In *Human Communication Theory,* edited by F. Dance. New York: Holt, Rinehart and Winston, 1967.
47. Jespersen, O. *How to Teach a Foreign Language.* London: George Allen and Unwin, 1904.
48. Johnson, F. C. *English as a Second Language: An Individualized Approach.* Brisbane, Australia: Jacaranda Press, 1973.
49. Joiner, E., and Westphal, P. *Developing Communication Skills.* Rowley, Mass.: Newbury House, 1978.
50. Kelly, L. G. *Twenty-Five Centuries of Language Teaching.* Rowley, Mass.: Newbury House, 1969.
51. Kochman, T., ed. *Rappin' and Stylin' Out: Communication in Urban Black America.* Chicago: University of Illinois Press, 1972.
52. Krashen, S. D. "The Monitor Model for Adult Second Language Performance." In *Viewpoints on English Language as a Second Language,* edited by Marina Burt, Heidi Dulay, and Mary Finocchiaro, pp. 152–61. New York: Regents, 1972.
53. Labov, W. *The Study of Non-Standard English.* Washington, D.C.: ERIC, Center for Applied Linguistics, 1969.
54. Lado, R. *Language Teaching: A Scientific Approach.* New York: McGraw-Hill, 1964.
55. _____. *Linguistics Across Cultures.* Ann Arbor: University of Michigan Press, 1957.
56. Lambert, W. "Psychological Approaches to the Study of Language." In *Teaching English as a Second Language,* edited by H. Allen. New York: McGraw-Hill, 1965.
57. Lee, W. R. *Language Teaching Games and Contests.* London: Oxford University Press, 1965.
58. Legarreta, D. "The Effects of Program Models on Language Acquisition by Spanish Speaking Children." *TESOL Quarterly* 13, no. 4 (1979).
59. Lenneberg, E. H., and Lenneberg, E., eds. *Foundations of Language Development.* New York: Academic Press, 1975.
60. _____. *Biological Foundations of Language.* New York: Wiley, 1967.
61. Lewis, G. "Bilingualism and Bilingual Education—The Ancient World to the Renaissance." In *Frontiers of Bilingual Education,* edited by B. Spolsky and R. Cooper. Rowley, Mass.: Newbury House, 1977.
62. Lozanov, G. *Suggestology and Outlines of Suggestopedy.* New York: Gordon and Breach, 1979.
63. Madson, H., and Bowen, J. *Adaptation in Language Teaching.* Rowley, Mass: Newbury House, 1978.

64. Moulton, W. G. *A Linguistic Guide to Language Learning.* 2d ed. New York: Modern Language Association, 1970.
65. _____. "Linguistics and Language Teaching in the United States, 1940–1960." In *Trends in European and American Linguistics,* edited by C. Mohemann, et al. Utrecht: Spectrum, 1961.
66. National Institute of Education. *Spanish-English Bilingual Education in the United States: Current Issues, Resources and Recommended Funding Priorities for Research.* Washington, D.C., 1975.
67. Nida, E. A. *Customs and Cultures.* New York: Harper, 1954.
68. _____. *Morphology: The Descriptive Analysis of Words.* Ann Arbor, Mich.: University of Michigan Press, 1949.
69. Oller, J. W., Jr., and Richards, J. C., eds. *Focus on the Learner: Pragmatic Perspectives for the Language Teachers.* Rowley, Mass.: Newbury House, 1973.
70. Oller, J., and Obrecht, D. H. "Pattern Drill and Communicative Activity: A Psycholinguistic Experiment," *IRAL* 6, no. 2 (1968): 165–72.
71. Paquette, F. A. "The Mandate for a National Program for Assessment of Language Proficiency." *ADFL* 11, no. 3 (1980); 12–15.
72. Paulston, C. B., and Bruder, M. N. *Teaching English as a Second Language: Techniques and Procedures.* Cambridge, Mass.: Winthrop, 1976.
73. _____ and _____. *From Substitution to Substance: A Handbook of Structural Pattern Drills.* Rowley, Mass. Newbury House, 1975.
74. _____. "Linguistic and Communicative Competence." *TESOL Quarterly* 8, no. 4 (1974): 347–62.
75. Pike, K. *Phonemics: A Technique for Reducing Languages to Writing.* Ann Arbor: University of Michigan Press, 1947.
76. Prator, C. "In Search of a Method." In *Readings on English as a Second Language,* edited by K. Croft. Cambridge, Mass.: Winthrop, 1980.
77. _____, and Robinett, B. W. *Manual of American English Pronunciation.* 3d ed. New York: Holt, Rinehart and Winston, 1972.
78. Quirk, R., and Greenbaum, S. *A Concise Grammar of Contemporary English.* New York: Harcourt Brace Jovanovich, 1973.
79. Richards, J. C., ed. *Understanding Second and Foreign Language Acquisition.* Rowley, Mass.: Newbury House, 1978.
80. Rivers, W. M. "Psychology and Linguistics as Bases for Language Pedagogy." In *Learning a Second Language.* 79th Yearbook of the National Society for the Study of Education. Chicago: University of Chicago Press, 1980.
81. _____, and Temperley, M. S. *A Practical Guide to the Teaching of English as a Second or Foreign Language.* New York: Oxford University Press, 1978.
82. _____. *Teaching Foreign-Language Skills.* Chicago: University of Chicago Press, 1968.
83. Robinett, B. W. *Teaching English to Speakers of Other Languages: Substance and Technique.* New York: McGraw-Hill, 1978.
84. _____. "The Domains of TESOL." *TESOL Quarterly* 6, no. 3 (1972): 197–207.
85. Sapir, E. *Language: An Introduction to the Study of Speech.* New York: Harcourt, Brace and Company, 1921.

86. Savignon, S. "Study of the Effect of Training in Communicative Skills as Part of a Beginning College French Course on Student Attitude and Achievement in Linguistic and Communicative Competence." Ph.D. dissertation, University of Illinois at Urbana-Champaign, 1971.
87. Saville-Troike, M. *Foundations for Teaching English as a Second Language: Theory and Method for Multicultural Education.* Englewood Cliffs, N.J.: Prentice-Hall, 1976.
87a. _____. *A Guide to Culture in the Classroom.* Rosslyn, Va.: National Clearinghouse for Bilingual Education, 1978.
88. Schermerhorn, R. A. *Comparative Ethnic Relations: A Framework for Theory and Research.* New York: Random House, 1970.
89. Schumann, J. H., and Stenson, N., eds. *New Frontiers in Second Language Learning.* Rowley, Mass.: Newbury House, 1975.
90. Shanker, Albert. Quoted in "Pay More, Get Less." *Forbes,* April 16, 1980: 35.
91. Shuy, R. W., and Fasold, R. W. *Language Attitudes: Current Trends and Perspectives.* Washington, D.C.: Georgetown University Press, 1973.
92. Sibelman, L. Address for the American Federation of Teachers at conference on "Bilingual Education: Ethnic Perspectives." Philadelphia: Nationalities Service Center, 1977.
93. Spolsky, B. *Educational Linguistics.* Rowley, Mass.: Newbury House, 1978.
94. _____, ed. *The Language Education of Minority Children.* Rowley, Mass.: Newbury House, 1972.
95. Stevick, E. W. *Adapting and Writing Language Lessons.* Washington, D.C.: Foreign Service Institute, 1971.
96. _____. *Teaching Languages: A Way and Ways.* Rowley, Mass.: Newbury House, 1980.
97. _____. *Memory, Meaning and Method: Some Psychological Perspectives on Language Learning.* Rowley, Mass.: Newbury House, 1976.
98. Strevens, P. *New Orientations in the Teaching of English.* Oxford: Oxford University Press, 1977.
99. Stuart, C. I. J. M. "Foreword" to *Introduction to the Handbook of American Indian Languages,* F. Boas. Washington, D.C.: Georgetown University Press, 1963.
100. Teitelbaum, H., and Hiller, R. J. "Bilingual Education: The Legal Mandate." *Harvard Educational Review* 47, no. 2 (1977): 142.
101. TESOL. *Guidelines for the Certification and Preparation of Teachers of English to Speakers of Other Languages in the United States.* Washington, D.C.: Georgetown University, 1975.
101a. _____. *Position Paper on the Role of English as a Second Language in Bilingual Education.* Washington, D.C.: TESOL, 1976.
101b. _____. *A Memo: Educating Children with Limited English.* Washington, D.C.: TESOL, n.d.
102. Thonis, E. W. *Teaching Reading to Non-English Speakers.* New York: Macmillan, 1970.
103. Valette, R. M. *Modern Language Testing.* 2d ed. New York: Harcourt Brace Jovanovich, 1977.

104. Van Ek, J. A. *The Threshold Level of Modern Language Teaching in Schools.* Longmans, 1978.
105. Velasquez, G. J. "Evaluation of a Bilingual Bicultural Education Program." Ph.D. dissertation, United States International University, 1974.
106. Wardhaugh, R. "Teaching English to Speakers of Other Languages: The State of the Art." Washington, D.C.: ERIC Clearinghouse for Linguistics, 1969. (ED 030119)
107. Whorf, B. L. *Language, Thought, and Reality.* Cambridge, Mass.: M.I.T. Press, 1956.
108. Widdowson, H. G. *Teaching Language as Communication.* London: Oxford University Press, 1978.
109. Wilkins, D. *Notional Syllabuses.* London: Oxford University Press. 1976.
110. Williams, F. "Language, Attitude, and Social Change." In *Language and Poverty: Perspectives on a Theme,* edited by Frederick Williams. Chicago Markham, 1970.
111. Winitz H., and Reeds, J. A., "Rapid Acquisition of a Foreign Language by Avoidance of Speaking." *IRAL* 11, no. 4 (1973): 295–317.
112. Yorkey, R. C. *Study Skills for Students of English as a Second Language* New York: McGraw-Hill, 1970.